The Smoke of Dreams

Reena Ribalow

NeoPoiesisPress.com

NeoPoiesis Press, LLC

2775 Harbor Ave SW, Suite D, Seattle, WA 98126-2138
Inquiries: Info@NeoPoiesisPress.com
NeoPoiesisPress.com

The Smoke of Dreams
ISBN 978-0-9975021-3-8 (pbk)
    1. Poetry. I. Ribalow, Reena.

LOC Number 2016909920

First Edition

Cover Design: Milo Duffin and Stephen Roxborough

Printed in the United States of America.

For Meir,
brother, other self,
perfect reader, believer,
companion of the soul and heart,
halfway through the wood
and beyond.

Contents

Part Three

Part One

An Ancient River of Blood

Jerusalem of Heaven, Jerusalem of Earth

I

I think this place may break my heart.

Around a corner lies the golden dome,
burnished to a postcard glow;
there a minaret rises
like an amazed breath.
But that's not where I am.
I am in these streets, narrow as a curse.
The buildings crouch like beggars,
their humbleness calculated
to make you give.
They do not intend to disappear.
Their windows are closed eyes
that refuse to open;
crossing their stony faces
is the mortality of laundry.
Under slanting rain, the roofs lie low,
resisting the pressure of the sky.
Soaring is not for those
bent by survival.

Clouds hang over like a doom.

Within the ramparts lies a heart of dust,
foreshadowing the rubble
into which they dream themselves:
crumbling under rafters
hanging in air,
like rails of a train
going nowhere.

There are nicer places.
There are gayer people:
not dressed in camouflage,
merging with the dun landscape,
passing as the meek of the earth.

3

There are places where
a dark descent of street
does not suggest
an ancient river of blood.

There are places where
the dank sad odor of life
does not lift as the rising hills ignite with lights:
where a crescent moon does not
cleave the heart
with the lucidity of vision:
where the cold, starred air
is not distilled
to the purity of revelation.

I think this place will break my heart.

II

This is the city of wounds.

On the Via Dolorosa pilgrims trace
the path of sacred sorrow:
church windows blossom a lacerated red.
Streets recall the name of martyred Jews:
the one whose flesh they flayed
because he would not damn the holy name:
the one whose torment in a Spanish cell
broke his body, not his faith.
Even children know the one
who sang the orphans toward the flames,
so they would not be afraid.

These wounds, and others that we bear,
are given to our children:
the sole inheritance
that they can count upon.

When the missiles fell,
we sealed the door with bleached cloths,
and taped the windows like injuries.
Our children, in their rubber masks,
knew which gas we really feared.
It burned their dreams,
like the tattooed numbers
on their forebears' arms.

We are covenanted to this fatal city,
which we claim.

On the street of the cafes,
bloodstains haunt the floors
and bullet holes mark the walls
like stigmata.
We suck pleasure through the coffee froth,
reach with sticky fingers
for the promised sweetness.

Through the dark transparency of night,
walls breathe out the musk of death.
Through veils of cigarette smoke,
we seek suspicious objects:
bound eternally
to implements of grief.
We worry our wounds,
probing the rawness, prolonging it.
When it hurts,
we know who we are.

Sangre de Cristo:
Blood of the Lamb:
the afflictions of Ishmael:
the sacrificial knife at Isaac's throat:
your mark on me, mine on you:
scars that testify where we've been,
and what we have visited on each other.

You do not live in Jerusalem
unless you love your wounds,
savor the salt of your blood,
surrender to suffering
in which all is absolved,
after which all is comprehended:
willing to be reborn,
generation upon generation,
in this land of eternal redemption,
in this city incandescent with pain.

III

The melodies of Mitteleurope ooze
through open windows,
like honey glaze.
Lamps cast golden light,
books climb to shadowed ceilings,
furniture holds its breath.
The sweetness of a long-forgotten village
settles on the sleepy street;
its leaves murmur of memories never known,
its trees bend toward secrets never told.

Crooked houses lean into each other.
A little box of tin and glass,
fastened to each gate,
celebrates the festival of light.

Candles flicker, declaring
their small miracles.

A bare bulb swings in a kitchen
redolent of many meals.
Walls are washed the blue
of Kurdistani skies,
Moroccan mountains,
valleys lost in legend.
On the window sill a glass jar

6

of pickles, ripening in their brine,
ready to sting the tongue
with the salt of tears.

Lemon blossoms drift upon the path.
Only the lemon tree
blossoms and fruits at once;
each bitter, fragrant sphere contains
what was and is to come.

Ancestral shades stir the dusky air.
On such nights,
a wanderer like me
is taken under
the benedictory palms
of a thousand nameless fathers,
and gathered in the arms
of countless mothers
warding off the dark.

Still Life

Edja in her pale rooms, divesting herself:
the walls tinted like the inside of shells
(tender and untouched).
Her shelves are ordered,
her counters stripped and wiped.
Refrigerator shelves glitter steel and light:
milk, yogurt, eggs incarnate white.

Cards crowd the kitchen wall,
mute voices calling her to Nadja's wedding,
Eva's party, the banquet honoring someone.
The telephone is dumb,
the couch sealed in plastic,
as if no one lived here,
as if already the shrouding had begun.

She sits on the floor,
around her scattered photographs:
pieces of a puzzle
that will never make a whole.

Here is Soraleh,
her face (that clever moon)
shadowed by the hat that never suited her:
Rosa, who died of diphtheria
before they knew how fortunate she was:
Max, lover of Chopin,
and the red-haired girl
who scorched his heart like flame,
Max, who married Anna in the end
and burned with her to bone:
and the cousins,
all the green-eyed children.

Edja in her pale rooms,
going through pictures,
divests herself.
She travels lightly,
emptying herself day by day,
for the journey home.

Blackout in Jerusalem

Our windows taped like wounds
against the light,
we wait within the star-cold
mouth of night.

(we silently explode into each other,
move through limbs and flesh,
while in the black
the little red fish dart
their hungry mouths now
fanged for pleasure)

Behind closed shutters
someone's dream snaps off.
The heart contains
the beat of falling bombs:
the burning bush
licks children with its tongues.

Rain

Leaves are gone or barely hanging on:
warm, it has been so warm.
Tables outdoors, coffee under umbrellas,
desert winds that cheat December,
denying winter.
Newspapers warn of dryness,
the aquifers drawing up the earth's poisons.
We have reached the bottoms of our wells;
one dare not draw so deep.

There is a price for any warm sweet interlude.
My daughter, dressed in black,
but mourning nothing,
tosses her untamed hair
at fear, at all my hints of doom.
Nothing can convince her:
not kitchen knives waiting to lash out at us
like serpent's tongues,
not the foretelling of gases (nerve, mustard, poison),
descending like rain from the inscrutable skies.

Perhaps of late I am too easily convinced
to pray for rain.

A familiar chill sets in;
the air is laden with the smell
of earth's deep moist need
and the scent of endings.

Absalom, My Son

He was beautiful, like you,
untamed as a wild horse
with a glory of hair.

When I watch you bent over a guitar,
hidden by your restless hair,
I am dazzled , like David ,
by the nimbus of your eclipsed face.

David's heart, flawed, duplicitous (like mine),
scorched by rage and passion,
chilled by calculation,
turned toward Absalom,
as toward the light.

I see your rebellious back
and understand how the old King
forgave the insurrection,
deflecting the blade meant to pierce him,
feeling the thrust of hatred
with his own fingertips,
and absolved the son's need
for the father's death.

It was Absalom caught in the trees
by his proud banner of hair
(that tender curtain between them, always)
that David could not bear.

I count soldiers' boots on every street,
dream of severed heads,
know in your eyes the burden of my dream.
"We'll die no matter what they do,"
you said once, and I wept
like David in his chamber,
"O my son, my son,
would God I could die for thee,
my son, my son."

From a Rooftop, Jerusalem

For Marshall

Parting seas of death and pine,
I excavate with mop and broom,
resisting miracles: opening tiled paths of blue,
as incandescent as the heart of flame.

Disintegration is not news to me.
Like you, I have been finely tuned toward fire.
With glittering pins the shared Romantic lie
has pinned you to your velvet setting:
there you blaze, with intricate
and fatal color, not yet sure enough to die.

These gold veined stones are luminous with scars,
their radiancy teaches me to be opaque.
Below me now, Jerusalem weaves on
her secret streets through mysteries of light.

Rainy Night Letter

For Stephen

I. The Letter

Just as these nights swell into morning,
and the clocks grow more violent,
you press into the room damply,
and the rain-beat soaks into the stones.

This has always been your hour.

I sit here writing letters.
Beneath the several skins we've grown and shed,
something deep and scarred as bone remains.
Between us we have been through wars and loss:
through countries: marriage: breakdown:
distance: love. And yet I write you letters
that begin and end, as formally as prayer.

II.   The Wedding

In a New York symmetry of grey,
you wandered like a refugee that day
I circled round him seven times;
over us a banner rose,
against the black Judean sky,
as heavy as the prayers that drew
an ancient rhythm from our tongues.
He ringed me in the garden
where the roses breathed:
the silken canopy dropped fringes
fragrant as the myrrh.

I did not think of you, or see you smashed,
transparent, frail, upon the grass
beneath his foot which, holy, ravaging,
destroyed the glass.

III. The Photograph Exhibition

The photographs of Hungary are dark,
and grainy as the naked pores of skin.
Hassidim sway, black flowers in the cave-like synagogue.
Their candles flicker in a passing wind: they pray.
Their huddled shadows cast upon the wall
a demon shape, as huge as they are small.

Somewhere then in Budapest, you were smaller still:
fragrant, camouflaged in lace, your wrist
unshaded by your father's blue tattoo.
Your mother watched your fingers woven
round her own, as flower-like as she could wish—
her blue-eyed, gentile flower.
She prayed against the dark.

And yet your photograph could stare at me
from these museum walls,
your eyes as blank as any ghetto child's.
In their stagnant pools, a world may end;
the blackness at their center calls me in.

Part Two

An Orphan Kiss

Cloisters

Walk the halls and suck the sadness in:
the sightless virgins on their marble knees,
the martyrs in their silent ecstasies,
each savoring his holiness alone
in cold and sweet severity of stone.

In spring the lilac hangs in purple clouds,
ripening the faint and sacred air:
lovers drifting, pair by pair,
seeking solace in the fragrant halls,
oblivious to unforgiving walls.

In winter a bleeding saint is one more dead,
flayed trees another suffering, against a sky of white.
Only the unborn, shadowless by arctic light,
walk the penitential, cobbled floors of stone,
welcoming in every cell, the chill of coming home.

Punic War

"The third Punic War between Rome and Carthage culminated in the razing of Carthage, which was utterly destroyed, and sown with salt to ensure nothing would grow there again."

It isn't far to Carthage:
just a turn
around his ear
into the shallow of his throat
and I fall
bent.

I saw the tarred road once,
through his eyes,
and I knew where it led.

I have too much of
slow unwinding yet
to risk the sticky black descent:

although my bland and milky tongue
would rake its furrows with
his sudden killing salt
if it were not that
once the salt is sown
there is no growing back
or coming home.

Night Fragment

Intricacies of line
from your eye to mine,
fit of bone
into bone.
Hollows catch,
and hold.
Protest of a palm
and the slow
slip of skin,
the low
bowing of the throat,
the splitting
of one whole
and hopeless
note.

After You

Summer will be the same.
I will walk linoleum squares
in the swollen August air,
grass blood on my
stained-glass feet.

At night, in my twisted sheet,
panting under slow,
seducing heat
it will be the same.

Only a vagrant pasture breath
will be left to cleave me
like the stroking of your lip

Memo to Myself

Note your phases:
you are near completion,
drawing full your tides
to shore.

Just that flooded hour.
You will lose the swell
and dwindle now:
diminished, patient,
pregnant as the moon.

Assimilation

We are left the ritual;
the love shudder is our prayer.
When the sky is mute
we light candles to an icon bed,
murmuring litanies of desire.

We count our rosaries
of old grievances.

I have become your Jew:
victim of your guilt, your absolution,
and the right to relive Friday's sin
on Sunday night.

The knife in alien hands
isolates the blood;
the centuries coagulate
against the foreign type.

The blood-lust is our heritage.

Song for Mark, without Music

You smelled of rainy trees,
I could not hold on.
It was only shaving lotion
and by evening it was gone.

your face lumped like pudding,
you bruised my mouth with tenderness:
an orphan kiss.
Afterwards we scrambled on our knees
for scattered pieces
of a meaning
absent from the start.

i tried
i needed you
who were you
when your hips erupted into mine
and your demented, overhanging face
desolated me
with blind and hungry eyes.

Your back was arrogant,
you rode my thighs,
we groaned the mutual
precision of our pain.

Your bedroom curtains blossomed,
fatal flowers promising
a poison that you
could not give.

My assenting blood
drew back your vampire lip;
but still I am denied the teeth,
the swoon, oblivion—
the victim's gift.

God is a bastard, too.
That's why I believe.

Devoured

Ah, your cupped palms;
I lie so small within.
My pale asphyxiated flesh
feeds the lust
of your solicitude.

Your love eliminates
the need for salt.

Prodigal Daughter

My grandmother cries about *Eugene Onegin*,
for faithfulness; she fears that it is lost.
And I am caught upon a pain
for worlds where no one screws,
but married people shut the door
and do what married people do.

This may be my undoing.

Your mouth is wet electric.
Yet one day I will turn and lock this door
against the melancholy nature of our flesh.
One last time I will descend your stairs,
and go to offer children to those tears.

Like a passing wound this room will seal.
When ceremony calls me virgin,
I will heal.

For Stephen, in Another Country

So much is left I never told you;
there are things I meant to say.

I dreamed we sat in a Hungarian café,
speaking in code:
your eyes to my mouth
my lips to your ear.
Your cigarette breathed
a message I could not penetrate.

I dreamed your memories:
a life in hiding (burrowed in your mother's scent):
mountain air , purifying tainted lungs:
ministering nuns, to cleanse
the fatal Jewish stain.

Under the gas lamps
we came together
as you'd always wished:
your heart freed
into its native tongue.

Your eyes singed me
with their bare blue need:
stripped to pain, they said
that I could never give enough.

Even in the dream we knew
there was a journey, a return,
another parting.

The rhythm of this earth tells me
things must spin to their close.
Sooner or later I will follow you
into the dark: again,
we will have travelled apart.

Cold Turkey

With the nonchalant contempt
of ghosts and dreams
you penetrate
my chain-choked door.
For three days I have lain
muffled in a blanket
red as blood.
It did not suffice
to mummify.
My belly throbs,
defenseless:
God, to groan
beneath your still
relentless bones.

Long Distance in the Laundromat

The air is savory with laundries;
leaning on an impotent machine,
I cry,
blurry and unfocused
as a washer's eye.

Intravenous consolation
trickles through
the detumescent wire.

I am adrift on disinfected seas;
simply for this minute
I decode
the message of a thousand
agitated loads.

Your Name Brushes By

Your ghost still flickers forth
on nights that hold the dark,
sweet threat of promise.
Your freckled fingers, vinelike,
choke your glass:
you swallow and breathe out
the warm sad fumes of hope.

It was all foretold when,
flylike, I was drawn
through summer haze
to share your smothered end.
Amid the drone of parakeets,
the fortune teller drew her cards;
your name did not appear.

The man I was not meant to wed
lies sleeping here beside me;
amid her bacon fumes he was denied.

But even then, in haunted heat
of dazzled white suburban streets,
you did not figure.

Only for this hour I am caught within
the dying blue-white gaslight of your eyes
before it's swallowed by
the living black October of the sky.

Love Song For Her Sleeping Husband

Carnations flower dryly.
I, too, sit in moderate flower,
pulsing to the tick
of an antique clock:
prince among the artifacts
of two o'clock.

Underneath synthetic fur
the floor is solid stone:
no earth but that allotted to each plant,
the dose for its survival,
and no more.

Three o'clock is graceful,
locking in its iron arabesques
the hours that came before.
Beyond, the darkened kitchen
glints with knives;
the sink is clogged with refuse
of some long forgotten tide.

Inside the room for living,
curtain-swathed,
the hours are passing landmarks
of the country that we keep—
the flowers, lamps and I—
beyond the secret circle of his sleep.

A little more:
the heater breathes its spurious warmth
into the hour of four.

Carnations flower dryly:
so do I,
with thin-stemmed hope
through nights that break and die.

Fourth Month Blues

Mama, my kitchen is plagued
with cockroaches;
I have no wide scarred shoe
like yours, that frightens
all the thin-legged hordes away.
Perhaps I'll learn your deadly art.

The jam jars stuffed with roses
sicken all my air with pink
domestic breath.

The lights are out all over.
Brooding on my terrace,
here above the city,
I am watchman, guardian,
mother.

In me now a heart is beating,
not my own;
my body swells and ebbs
to latent tides.

I sit here hoarding stars
and fingering silence,
no longer profligate:
preserving moments in the single dark,
like summer cherries
canned for winter stock.

Marital Thoughts in a Jerusalem Café

Cigarette-seeded flowerpots,
dry, inimical to growth;
only newspapers flower here.
Neither Hebrew, Russian, French
brings us news we do not know.

Inside, we wait.
Through open doors the sunlight falls,
regardless, on the doomed,
and those who will not grant the doom.
These my people, so I'm told,
each locked in prophecies
of solitary coffee cups.

The sadness of a drooping orange sock,
the slight, dark bodies
alien to my own—
against them there is no denial I may work,
no exile sets me free.

Although your absent spirit
haunts this hour:
hard, malignant as this
flowerless flowerpot of earth,
you are my promised portion:

I am covenant-bound
to work our desert,
faithful, visionary,
till it blooms.

The Moon's Truth

(before the war)

My plants are moonstruck.
Moon dusts their uplifted palms.
Onto the terrace sifts the pallid light:
on rooftops, on the puppet cars,
a winter-colored, phosphorescent breath.

My womb is moon-seared
and its moonscapes, flat as death.
In lunar rays the mind is bent
to mutant shapes.

Only missiles will flower overhead,
their moment's purgatory paling to
a fatal radiance of white.

Epithalamion: For My Husband, On the Impending Marriage of his Estranged Friend

Last night you heard he's marrying.
At last, so fast, *schlemiel*:
who dwindled to a trail of fading footsteps
leading backward.
So many nights you've tracked them
through the rooms you knew,
still hung with all that hope,
hazy as the pale forbidden smoke
of stolen cigarettes.

The streetlamps hang in heavy flowers:
the streets of Queens proceed like prison numbers.
In them still, your sweet slight ghosts run free.

Across a motionless expanse
we may as well call oceans,
there are no signals sent by one who
whistled underneath your window,
and no answer lent from one who
threw a twisted rope of sheets
and drew him in.

The nights you spun have caught the moment.
There it lies, embalmed: a wedding gift,
so fragile, dead, and true.

Black Night of the Heart in the Café Atara

I bought flowers in the street, then;
now they have the scent
of the visited grave.

Wine-drenched afternoons,
curtains flapping against a cloudless sky,
our skins wet with the essence of us:
café conversations launched us,
sweetly to sail the starry nights.

Your eyes are a distant light
across a black and empty field.
I am weary of battle, of this tiny
seething universe of self.
The poisonous insects devour our souls:
pain, rage, fear, life-terror.

I am your accomplice,
your death vessel;
I bear our nullity within me,
like a child.

I do not consent.

I would be an empty vessel.
Through me let talk, laughter,
cigarette smoke, clashing plates,
sweetness disappearing on the tongue,
the momentary touch
of fingers flow;
through me let life find its path.

Part Three

After it All is the Wind

Domestic Enchantment

Some spells turn a prince into a frog,
some tame wild girl to wife,
conjure mother out of woman,
tranced by cooking, tending, laundry.

Swaying from their pegs the colored clothes
are dazzling as the wings of
subjugated butterflies.
Sun scents the air with opiate of soap;
captivity subdues the blood like sleep,
with cleanly, sweet,
obliterating peace.

The kitchen table is set
with the artifacts of enchantment:
a jug of flowers upon a blue-checked cloth,
white mugs, a fresh-baked cake.
She herself prepared the potion,
self-bewitched,
the recipe her mother's song,
sung before memory.

A cup of flour, two eggs,
a handful of the magic
that fetters sense and soul:
that gilds the room the gold
of an imagined sun:
that heats her veins
like the tea which steams
from teapots,
with the smoke of dreams.

When My Grandfather Died

"Well," my aunt said. "We're next, kid."
I had already been notified,
by the smell I could not name or bear
rising from his bed:
by his naked voice calling
"*Vas is die stunde?*",
pursuing the hour
as time withdrew from him :
by the hospital sheets lettered
like the scrolls which told his life,
striped like the *talit*,
in which he grew to his absolute size—
Rabbi, High Priest—
in which he would be
smally laid
under dry and holy earth.

In death, as in all else,
my Grandmother prepared the way,
so he could worry about
more important things.

He would bring her
the gift of himself
in his own time.

"*Vie der alter Yid hert nit,* " she used to say,
but he heard now.

He ceased to call me
even by my mother's name.
"*Rivka, ich kum.*"
He knew where he was going,
keeping a promise to her
for once.

Glossary of Yiddish Phrases

Vas is die stunde? — "What time is it?" or, literally, "What is the hour?"

Vie der alter Yid hert nit — "How this old man doesn't hear." or, literally, "How this old Jew doesn't hear."

Ich kum — "I'm coming."

Dorit Disguised: To My Student, At the School Fair

Separated by a crazy quilt of hawkers, clowns and mimes
who only yesterday impersonated students:
of milling parents fingering the merchandise
in search of secrets that their children took away:
by the eight years between us, you and I:
you wave to me from the stone bridge—
your moat, which isolates enchanted things
from those who've left (or never known) its grace,
who linger in this dim, uncertain place.

This is a message, sent to you across these sunlit heads:
one last lesson taught your teacher, as I watch you
move, unknowing, in its knowing light.

The harlequin you've painted on has caught you
in the sorrow of its art; through its prophecy, you glow.
And though you move, its destiny dispelled,
I see the shade enweave your shining hair,
as smilingly, you leave your bridge and come across to me.

Winter Street with Figure

There is always a middle-aged woman
carrying bags through the rain.
Her shoulders are bent under the weight
of bread, milk, and a celery
whose tail waves limply at her side,
like a dog that is tired, too.

She looks ahead,
but you can tell she does not see
the slick street, the trees dripping down
on her impervious shoulders:
the houses cruelly winking their warm lights
at anyone walking the cold streets.

Her eyes see something else,
and her lips are pressed together
against what might escape.

She is carrying a dying mother in her,
a sick marriage, a cat with a tumor,
a son who will not smile,
a faucet that will not stop dripping,
a daughter lost to a bleak love,
and a bank account that is her enemy.

For a moment she may look
at the young girl drifting
down the rainy street,
water gathering in her hair like jewels.
She may remember her own rain-clouded hair,
the drops splintering
at the touch of his hand.

She may remember this,
she may not.
She may not be able to name all she carries:
probably she does not know
that she is that middle-aged woman

with the head-scarf
who is caught in the rain,
always with bags in her hands.

Through the Kitchen Window
by Northern Light

Autumn, Scotland

Behind the sky of afternoon, broods the dark.
Here you trap light as you'd trap a hummingbird:
your net quick, and precise.

Winds bend what will bend;
the cat on the wall is
a grey resistant ball
waiting for this to pass.

The washing machine behind me whines
like a child who needs me, needs me, needs me.

Out there things are dropping, baring.
The trees let go, covering the earth
in the brilliant colors of their loss.

Reizl the Mad: On a Story by I.B. Singer

Her madness is pure as the veins
of the fired vessel:
shattered and whole,
consumed by pain.

Under moons and leaking roofs,
they dance the dance of truth:
goblins, shades and imps of three o'clock.
This is the hour when all are lost,
that turns us into what we are.

Daylight wanderer of alien streets,
her tongue is numbed by language
cold, precise as winter light.
Her eyes are of the night,
her back is curved;
untutored in her bending ways
the straight-spined break.

She looses hungry Yiddish syllables.
Their rhythm beats
like blood within our veins.

Her curses blaze across the room,
and light it with their
stubborn, knowing flame.

This ravaged, tender place we fear,
she inhabits and contains,
for all our sakes.

Winter of Discontent: Jerusalem

Over it all is the wind.

Walls crumble from damp.
The damp rises, perhaps from the earth:
from underground cisterns:
from sources too deep to name.

Yesterday a mouse stood twitching
in the living room, waiting for a sign.
They say when you dig to build,
the mice emerge from their ruined burrows,
confusing the secret with the public,
seeking darkness in the wrong places.
Their nerves tell them they do not belong here;
but until their compass points them back
to their subterranean lives,
daily we catch the scent of decay,
of things we wish we did not know.
We live with mice
lurching through the kitchen at dinnertime,
hiding in the burners,
on the brink of flame.

Under it all is the wind.

Across the lightless road,
an Arab man in his *keffiyeh*.
They say a red one means one thing, a green another.
His means I cannot see him:
only his eyes across the Hebron Road,
and those an illusion.
The rain washes down the road:
cars with blind eyes pass us.
Will he lift his arm against me?
Do I see him, or only myself?
The road rises between us like a river;
we watch across its banks.
He unwraps his *keffiyeh*, exposing a face.

I follow my path, offering him a back.
When I turn he is gone.
I am still here, for now.

Through it all is the wind.

It rains and rains.
Once it snowed.
Twice, hail clattered down like bullets.
The Galilee is rising.
Last winter was dry;
now there is more water
than we know how to use.
The overflow pours
toward the Dead Sea,
transforming into absolute mineral.

Our drinking water grows pure:
the plants are plotting extravagant growth:
ants and mosquitoes refuse to die.

The rain seeps through cracks,
it pools on the floor,
it stains the walls.
They say water doesn't need
a direct path;
it finds its way in,
following us everywhere,
and you can never know for sure
how it will finish,
and where it began.

After it all is the wind.

Raisins and Almonds

She was across the street, hanging
the frayed underwear of her withered husband.
He cast on her a malevolent eye.
Her frail head, bobbing like a dandelion:
white tufted hair and a soft webbed face,
smiling, for reasons no one could see.
She washed plastic bags,
hanging them to dry, in gaping mouths,
fed the wild cats remains
of pale, parsimonious dinners.

A death notice posted on the gate:
Beloved Husband of...
She ventured out to sit on the steps, then,
where the sun fell , lifting her face
like a starved bird.

She sang a lullaby : Raisins and Almonds,
sleep little boy sleep.
No children, she said, not after Siberia.
Her voice was cracked paper. She smiled.

Then she was gone, leaving only
a vagrant bag to drift the street,
and the cats to grieve.

To Another Poet Growing Old

For Anita B.

It might have been the same road Robert Frost wandered,
thinking, "One could do worse than be a swinger of birches."
We did not intend swinging from branches.
We ran that empty Vermont road in conquest,
laying claim to Breadloaf Mountain,
shouting to the non-existent traffic,
"Don't run us over!
We are the future of American Literature."
At eighteen you believe these things.

We did not know then what it takes to be
even the smallest stitch in the future
of anything.

I saw your picture, forty years later,
grey hairs weaving their way through
the dark cloud of hair,
fine lines scoring your skin:
spider webs,
patiently and intricately spun
to trap their prey.

You've won prizes,
I've won prizes:
yours outweigh mine.
As "for destruction" (Frost again),
I wouldn't know,
but when it comes to grief,
I'd bet we're pretty even.

It says you're a peace activist.

I've lived through wars, through almost-wars:
carried brown paper cartons
with gasmasks for my children.
I've heard the gunshots from my bedroom window,
and figured their direction:

felt explosions that shake the air into shocked silence:
waited to count the ambulances' wails
(how many tells you how bad it was).
I called, like everyone, on telephone lines
clotted like damaged veins,
to see if anyone I loved was there.

Most of those whose scattered body parts
were meticulously gathered for burial,
prayed for peace.

You are a mother and grandmother.
So am I.
But those are words like Chinese letters,
where a picture represents a story.

If we met today
what would we call out;
what faith could join us?
Only that we ran that road
(and probably still do)
wanting the same thing:
for someone reading somewhere
to understand,
and know that we were here.

The Many-colored Dress

For Rori

The Spanish fan I gave you,
with its painted tale of
mythic birds and flowers,
you were saving for a ball.
Wrapped in scarves, you dreamed yourself
down shimmering halls, through doors
that opened into dazzled rooms
where you danced your heart's rhythm.

They hurled names at you in the street:
the balls waned, like dying moons.
You wore your pink sweat suit,
like a hurt.
Just there, childhood ends:
when you are nothing
but yourself.

Now you search the world,
for the remnants of your dream:
your life a secret lived
on the dark side of your moon.

Inside my closet, the dress I bought you:
vivid as a rare bird's wing.
Its pattern hides a tiny flaw,
impossible to see.
But I know it is there.

Last night I dreamed the many-colored dress
rose up from its cupboard ,
telling me I must bear
its winged colors and unmendable hole:
remain engorged with the ungiven:
and diminish to nothing
but myself.

The Broken World

> "Then from Endless Light a single line
> hung down…into that space and through
> that line he emanated, created, formed
> and fashioned all the worlds."
>
> From *The Tree of Life*
> Rabbi Isaac Luria
> 16th Century Kabbalist

Gravity is against us.
Plates, lamps, limbs
yearn toward destruction.

Things pull to their own shattering.

Holding on is the struggle,
patching minute to minute,
mending the shattered hours.
Light casts deceptive patterns in the void:
but enchantment ends.
At the edge of anything,
the blackness waits,
ineradicable.

Roofs strive, foundations thrust
toward the absolute;
the ground convulses in its lust to erupt.
Edge clashes against edge seizing,
in an agony of imperfection.

Bedrock cracks.

Our lives are built on a fault;
through the dust, the dismemberment,
completion is sought.

Desert Light

Was it Cezanne who said, "God is light,"
and went South to paint?
Or was it someone else who did not know
that we can take only so much light,
without going crazy?
The slant of afternoon in a dim room,
the dazzle after a passing cloud,
a radiance through shifting leaves,
is all that we can bear.

Here people are mad with light,
their nerves raw with it,
their eyes irradiated ;
they cannot see right.
Shadows disappear from streets
without dimension,
with nowhere to hide.
Light hunts us down,
relentless as the Law.

Some plants survive, some thrive,
some play dead by noon light,
wakening to moist life
in the seducing dark.

The light of Europe hints,
suggesting immanence.
Civility infuses light:
the safety of umbrellas, of cloudy parks,
of rooms that hold their breath,
gilded with motes of gold;
this is easy, this wears well.

The prophets were born to desert light,
crazed with it, dooming us
to a surfeit of holiness.

We endure, odd growths
on a sun-battered land.
Saints, madmen, artists
offer their strange and mutant fruit.
Eat of it, they plead,
and know in every cell
the terrible truth:
that God is everywhere.

Another Tree Poem

All these poems about trees .
This one is outside the window of my rented apartment,
where I am not unpacked :
as if I had not decided to live here yet.

The tree was there when I got the call;
my brother had let go his ravaged body,
released the death sonnets
from his swollen hands.
At sunset I saw his light
rise from the leaves ,
signaling me one last time.

Winter winds stripped the tree,
a week-long storm bent it,
snow and hail splintered branches;
it was a tropical tree, not made for this.
I thought it would never recover.

That winter I lost something like love,
rising in my veins like sap—
from dormancy, to blossom, to blight.
I was Millay's lonely winter tree,
its birds vanished one by one,
its boughs more silent than before.

In autumn my father followed the foliage
from its pale beginnings
to its deepest burgundy leaf-blood,
colors spilling over the Vermont mountains.
Not that last summer,
when his skin yellowed, tinged by brown,
like a leaf tuning itself toward extinction.
He left behind the snaps of
himself , the chasm of his eyes,
and the careful photographs of trees
burning themselves out along the hills.

With a book of Russian poetry
my grandmother sat under a Bronx tree,
transformed into Pushkin's greening oak:
in its branches a cat telling tales, a mermaid,
and her dead husband's face,
trapped, elusive as the moon.
She called it her dreaming tree,
here long before her,
and long after.

My mother's deadly stroke
twisted her like a broken bird;
she turned to me her blind eye,
uttered incomprehensible syllables,
the language of ancient wounds.
Through my window the leaves
trembled like loss.

This poem is about myself: poems always are.
It may tell you how the tree put out feathery shoots,
briefly filled the window with yellow flowers
like fleeting suns,
that it still bears withered branches,
though some of them bud green,
bound as they are to a living tree.

It's another poem about another tree,
or a poem about myself,
or a poem about enduring,
until we don't.

Thank You

Above all, to my parents, Harold U. Ribalow and Shoshana Shuck Ribalow, who taught us that the life of the imagination was a privilege, with art its greatest gift, and who gave us the courage to live in the light of our own truths.

To Emanuel Green for illuminating the dark, and insisting all the way that the answer was, "Write".

To Anita Kamien for being the sister I never had, and for seeing me through it all.

To Sharon Pomerantz, and Patricia Randell for reading my manuscript and responding with profound perception and generosity. And to Bonnie MacDougall for journeying with me through the past and through the poems, with the comprehension of a true reader, and the instincts of a true friend.

To my gracious editor, Dale Winslow, who nurtures her garden and her poets: for who and what she is.

To my two children, Riora and Shaiel, the best of my "creations": for being in the world, and in my life.

And again and always, to my brother, Meir Z. Ribalow, whose love, faith, and dedication through the years made it possible to release the magic in the words and within myself.

Acknowledgements

"Jerusalem of Heaven, Jerusalem of Earth", "Marital Thoughts in a Jerusalem Café", published in *The Jerusalem Review*

"Jerusalem of Heaven, Jerusalem of Earth", published in "Winning Writers .com"(First Prize , Margaret Reid Poetry Contest)

"Still Life", published in *Voices, Israel*

"Blackout in Jerusalem", published in *Ariel*

"Rainy Night Letter", published in *Shirim*

"Punic War", "Night Fragment", "After You", "Cloisters", "Song for Mark", published in *The Literary Review*

"Prodigal Daughter", "Cold Turkey", published in *Arc*

"Memo to Myself", published in *English Poetry from Israel*

"Long Distance in the Laundromat", published in *English Poetry from Israel*

"Air Persists", published in *English Poetry from Israel*

"Your name Brushes By", published in *The Keats Prize Anthology*

"Lovelorn Song for Her Sleeping Husband", published in *The Keats Prize Anthology (Honorable Mention for Keats Poetry Prize)*

"From a Rooftop, Jerusalem", published in *The Jewish Frontier*

"Fourth Month Blues", published in *The New York Quarterly*

"Black Night of the Heart in the Café Atara", published in *The Jerusalem Post*

"Domestic Enchantment", published in *Voices, Israel*

About the Author

Reena Ribalow is a poet and writer living in Jerusalem, Israel. She was born in New York City and educated at the Yeshiva of Central Queens, Hunter College High School and Queens College. She attended the University of Iowa PhD. Program and Writer's Workshop on a Danforth Foundation Fellowship.

She is First Prize winner of the *Moment Magazine-Karma Foundation Short Fiction Contest*, the *Margaret Reid Poetry Prize* and *The Golden Prize*. Other awards include the *Keats Poetry Prize*, the *Stand Magazine International Short Story Competition*, and *The New River* poetry prize. "Winter Street With Figure" was a finalist for the *Cutthroat Joy Harjo Poetry Award*; "Voices of the Dead" was a finalist for *Cutthroat's Rick DeMarinis Short Story Award*, and appears in *Cutthroat's* Fifth Anniversary Edition. Her work has been published in *The Jerusalem Review: Ariel: The New York Quarterly: Shirim : The Literary Review: Midstream: The Jerusalem Post: The Keats Prize Anthology: Voices, Israel: Arc* and *Israel Short Stories* among others.

Her grandfather was Menachem Ribalow, essayist, Hebraist and founder and editor of *Hadoar*, the first Hebrew weekly in America. For the past thirty-five years she has been a Chief-Screener for the prestigious Harold U. Ribalow Prize for Jewish Fiction, named in honor of her father, Anglo-American Jewish critic, editor and anthologist, Harold U. Ribalow, and administered by Hadassah Magazine. Her grandfather on her maternal side was an Orthodox Lithuanian rabbi. This heritage, its memories and echoes, a previous marriage into a Holocaust survivor family, as well as an adult life rooted in Israel, form the blood knot of her writing.

NeoPoiesis: *a new way of making*

1) in ancient Greece, poiesis referred to the process of making: creation - production - organization - formation - causation

2) a process that can be physical and spiritual, biological and intellectual, artistic and technological, material and teleological, efficient and formal

3) a means of modifying the environment and a method of organizing the self, the making of art and music and poetry, the fashioning of memory and history and philosophy, the construction of perception and expression and reality

4) an independent publisher with a steadfast goal to print and promote outstanding poets, writers and artists that reflect the creative drive and spirit of the new electronic landscape

NeoPoiesisPress.com